At the Museum

by Rachel Johns
illustrated by Stephen Axelsen

SCHOOL PUBLISHERS

Printed in China

ISBN 10: 0-15-351433-7
ISBN 13: 978-0-15-351433-3

Ordering Options
ISBN 10: 0-15-351212-1 (Grade 2 Advanced Collection)
ISBN 13: 978-0-15-351212-4 (Grade 2 Advanced Collection)
ISBN 10: 0-15-358068-2 (package of 5)
ISBN 13: 978-0-15-358068-0 (package of 5)

4 5 6 7 8 9 10   0940   15 14 13 12 11 10 09

Characters

Teacher

Director

Mr. Fowler
(Director's assistant)

Anthony

Madison

Setting: At the museum

Teacher: Good morning, Director. Thank you for meeting with my students.

Director: I'm glad you could come. This is my assistant, Mr. Fowler.

Anthony: We'd like to ask you some questions about the dinosaur exhibition coming in May.

Madison: Then we're going to report back to our classmates.

Teacher: You start, Anthony.

Anthony: Why did you decide to have a dinosaur exhibition?

Director: Dinosaurs were amazing animals. Even though they became extinct long ago, people are still fascinated by them.

Teacher: That's true. Our students are!

Mr. Fowler: Kids can't get enough of dinosaurs.

Madison: Do you have any other extinct creatures in your exhibition?

Director: We did think carefully about including other creatures, but it wasn't feasible. There isn't room in the museum!

Anthony: Where did you get the exhibits?

Director: Other museums around the world loaned us their exhibits.

Mr. Fowler: My job was to contact the museums to see whether they were able to contribute to our exhibition.

Madison: How did you start?

Mr. Fowler: I exchanged e-mails and letters with the other museums. Hundreds of letters and e-mails were delivered to museums around the world.

Director: We were really pleased by the response. We thought organizing an exhibition like this would be difficult to accomplish.

Anthony: What kinds of things will be included?

Mr. Fowler: We have several dinosaur skeletons. We're also creating an area that will show what the world was like when dinosaurs were alive. There will be displays about different kinds of dinosaurs, too.

Director: We even have life-size dinosaur models.

Madison: What do you hope to achieve with this exhibition?

Director: Museums serve the community. We hope this dinosaur exhibition will bring people to the museum who have never been before.

Anthony: Can you tell us more about how the exhibition will be set up?

Director: We have plenty of helpers at the museum. They will show people around and talk about the exhibits.

Mr. Fowler: Some of the exhibits are interactive, so people can get really involved.

Director: We even have an area with comfortable chairs. Going to museums can be fun, but it can be tiring, too! We're serious about looking after our visitors.

Anthony: Will there be many school groups coming to the exhibition?

Mr. Fowler: We hope that all the local schools will attend. We have sent information packets to them.

Teacher: Then you are expecting a lot of people.

Mr. Fowler: Yes, we are expecting a big crowd every day.

Madison: Do you hope to have more exhibitions like this in the future?

Director: People have different personalities, so they like different things. We're asking people who come to see the dinosaurs to tell us what else they would like to see.

Anthony: Finally, what is your favorite dinosaur exhibit?

Mr. Fowler: I must admit that I love the *Tyrannosaurus rex* skeleton.

Director: I agree, though it is extremely scary!

Anthony: Thank you. We have plenty to report back to our class.

Madison: We'll be back again in May to see the exhibition.

Teacher: I can't wait!

Think Critically

1. What words would you use to tell about Mr. Fowler?

2. Where did the exhibits at the museum come from?

3. What tells you that this story is a Readers' Theater?

4. What did Madison and Anthony want to find out about?

5. Would you like to go to a dinosaur exhibition? Why or why not?

 **Social Studies**

Write a Paragraph The story is set in a museum. Write a paragraph about why museums are important to communities.

School-Home Connection Talk about the book with a family member. Then talk about what the world was like when dinosaurs were alive.